TO EACH HIS HOME

To Each His Home

INSPIRED INTERIORS AS UNIQUE AS THEIR OWNERS

Bilyana Dimitrova

PRINCETON ARCHITECTURAL PRESS   NEW YORK

PUBLISHED BY
PRINCETON ARCHITECTURAL PRESS
37 EAST SEVENTH STREET
NEW YORK, NEW YORK 10003

FOR A FREE CATALOG OF BOOKS, CALL 1-800-722-6657
VISIT OUR WEBSITE AT WWW.PAPRESS.COM

EDITOR: NANCY EKLUND LATER
DESIGNER: PAUL WAGNER

SPECIAL THANKS TO: NETTIE ALJIAN, SARA BADER,
DOROTHY BALL, NICOLA BEDNAREK, JANET BEHNING,
BECCA CASBON, CARINA CHA, PENNY (YUEN PIK) CHU,
RUSSELL FERNANDEZ, PETE FITZPATRICK, WENDY FULLER,
JAN HAUX, CLARE JACOBSON, AILEEN KWUN, LINDA LEE,
AARON LIM, LAURIE MANFRA, KATHARINE MYERS,
LAUREN NELSON PACKARD, JENNIFER THOMPSON,
ARNOUD VERHAEGHE, JOSEPH WESTON, AND
DEB WOOD OF PRINCETON ARCHITECTURAL PRESS
—KEVIN C. LIPPERT, PUBLISHER

LIBRARY OF CONGRESS CATALOGING-IN-
    PUBLICATION DATA
DIMITROVA, BILYANA.
    TO EACH HIS HOME : INSPIRED INTERIORS AS UNIQUE
AS THEIR OWNERS / BILYANA DIMITROVA. — 1ST ED.
    P.   CM.
    ISBN 978-1-56898-796-5 (ALK. PAPER)
    1. INTERIOR DECORATION—PSYCHOLOGICAL ASPECTS.
I. TITLE.
    NK2113.D56 2008
    747—DC22   2008015339

It's like we were preprogrammed,

LIKE BIRDS MAKING THEIR NESTS.

We were just born knowing that

WE HAVE TO GET THE TWIGS AND

bring them to the tree and add the mud.

WE JUST HAVE TO DO IT.

—JESSICA GRINDSTAFF

CONTENTS

ACKNOWLEDGMENTS

First and foremost, I'd like to thank the people whose homes appear in this book for giving me the opportunity to create. Just as they so freely express their creativity at home, they allowed me to express and indulge my own. I will be eternally grateful to them for letting me in and giving me a large embrace.

I'd like to thank my editor, Nancy Eklund Later, for liking this book from the start and not having a doubt in her mind that I would get it published. It's rare for two likes to find each other, and I am thankful to have found her. I'd like to thank my design team at Princeton Architectural Press, Paul Wagner and Deb Wood, for their careful translation of my ideas and for their creative input.

I'd like to thank my mother, Albena, for her unwavering confidence in me as an artist. I'd like to thank her and my father, Ludmil, for introducing me to art at an early age through their own work, be it smelling the oil paint at home or seeing my dad's witty political cartoons. Their artistic talents are a continued source of inspiration for me. I'd also like to thank my husband, Edward Mullen, the love of my life, my best friend, and my most loyal companion, who keeps me strong and happy. Everything seems better and nothing seems as bad when he's by my side. Words cannot express how deeply grateful I am for his infinite love and support. I'd like to thank my friends and extended family for their care and encouragement along the way, and my thirteen-year-old brother, Constantine, for his wonderment when looking at my photographs.

I'd like to thank my first photography teacher, Ann Currier, at Fiorello H. LaGuardia High School, who sprouted my love for the medium, and my professors Stephen Shore, for his considered formalism, and Larry Fink, for his passion and drive, and for his continued friendship and guidance. They inspired me with their work and showed me what to strive for.

I'd like to thank Stacy Schwartz for hiring me to shoot for the *Village Voice*, which allowed me to meet Tami Lee on assignment. I'd like to thank Sara Barrett at the *New York Times* House & Home section for helping me contact Lenny Weiner, and *Metropolis* magazine for helping me contact Peter Rittmaster.

And last but not least, I'd like to thank Louis Diep, at Hong Digital Color Inc., for creating the impeccable scans that fill the pages of this book.

INTRODUCTION

"I couldn't imagine living in a home like that!" This is the reaction people often have to the houses featured in this book. Our ideas are so different when it comes to how we want our homes to look. And why shouldn't they be? As Mija Bankava, the creator of one of the interiors featured here, explains, "If you really put your personality into creating your home, why should others feel comfortable with it?"

The owners of the spaces illustrated here all described to me an instinct to make the spaces they live in their own. They said they could never live in a home decorated by someone else. They gravitate toward the handmade over the store-bought, and their homes are filled with unique objects of personal value. Rather than use their homes as places to display their material possessions (and by extension, their "good taste," status, or wealth), they see them as places to display aspects of their character, their personal history, and even their ideals.

When seeing the first of these homes, I was astounded by how instantaneously I was pulled into the world of its owners. Roderick Sykes and Jacqueline Alexander-Sykes didn't have to say a word: St. Elmo Village so strongly communicated who they are that it did all the talking for them. I became addicted immediately to the warmth and intimacy that this small cluster of bungalows exuded. I was in such awe of Roderick and Jacqueline's vision for the village, and so appreciative of the time and effort that went into creating it, that I decided to make a record of their home.

As a photographer, I have sought to record how people personalize the spaces they inhabit, and how those inanimate spaces come to life because of the human touch. I started by photographing people's front porches and backyards in Upstate New York and then began venturing inside. I wanted to photograph the unmade bed, the sink full of dishes—the evidence of human presence. I wanted to take this interest further and document not only how people personalize their homes unintentionally, by simply using their space, but also how people do this in a much more intentional and considered way.

At about the same time, I also began working in the field of architectural photography. I enjoyed the process of documenting a single building or interior in depth, examining it from different angles and distances. I liked the implied importance given to something when shown in more than one photograph. So while photographing what professional designers created, I became even more interested in finding homes that were created just as intensely by the homeowners themselves. It wasn't until St. Elmo Village that I found what I was looking for.

I felt driven to seek out and photograph more homes like St. Elmo Village that showed the magnitude of what ordinary people can create. I wanted to capture these homes for myself, but also as a record for the homeowners. This became paramount when I was photographing Tami Lee's apartment in Brooklyn, New York, as she told me that her landlord was forcing her out. I couldn't believe that a home like hers, so carefully decorated with layer upon layer of personal objects, would cease to exist. Tami's was the second home that I photographed, and after that, I began to think of my pictures as a way to preserve these and other incredible homes where self-expression trumped all other design considerations.

My search culminated in documentation of the eight homes presented in this book. They were each decorated in such a deliberate and thoughtful way that I chose to photograph them faithfully, without moving or rearranging a thing.

The homeowners supported my efforts, often leaving me alone to work and allowing me to come back if I needed more time. Their walls constantly invited conversation, the purposefully arranged objects engaging me and piquing my interest. But while I worked, I was quiet and focused. When it came time to look at the final photographs with the homeowners, my questions flowed freely, and they were all happy to entertain them. Like their homes, their answers were personal and revealing. I decided to include their words alongside my photographs because they illuminate just how much their homes are of them, and how much they are of their homes.

To the last, the homeowners are secure in who they are and in their ability to express themselves fully at home. Their homes are as unique as they are, and so transcend conventional ideas of "home." Erik Sanko and Jessica Grindstaff's apartment is a seamless coming together of their two tastes, melted down into one unified vision; Bottle Village provides a way for its original owner, Grandma Prisbrey, to live on after her death; Mija Bankava's loft is one big canvas composed as she would one of her paintings; Peter Rittmaster's summerhouse exists to give pleasure to its guests; St. Elmo Village is a home for the community, built by the community; Tami Lee's apartment represents a particular moment in her personal life; Lenny Weiner's apartment is a dream home, created through the sheer force of imagination; Larry Fink and Martha Posner's house is secondary to the environment that surrounds it, and it's that environment that they call home.

Each space differs in appearance and tells different stories about its owner, but it's what they had in common that drew me to them. Throughout my search I saw many homes that were very original in their decor, but the dedication to expressing a highly personal vision as well the heightened consideration for all things incorporated in the home were not always present. The homeowners in this book all share an ease in expressing themselves: for them, decorating their homes is second nature. After photographing their spaces, I always felt compelled to ask the same question: "Was this a lot of work for you?" All responded in the same way: they didn't see it as work in the traditional sense (one even called it a guilty pleasure). These homeowners all seem driven to engage with their living environments. As a result they create one-of-a-kind spaces—beautiful sanctuaries, to which they can't wait to return.

I am grateful to have been allowed a close look at what these homeowners find beautiful. Their homes have inspired me to look to myself first, before looking elsewhere, for inspiration and to have faith in my own ideas. Each demonstrates, through his or her home, an unabashed indulgence in being yourself, doing it yourself, and not caring about what others think of you. For me, their beauty lies in that uplifting and invigorating call.

Erik Sanko & Jessica Grindstaff's Tribeca Apartment

Erik Sanko has lived in this apartment since his youth. While living there alone in his thirties, he was joined by Jessica Grindstaff. They married and now share the apartment with their dog, Horse. Erik is a member of the band Skeleton Key and a marionette maker. Jessica is an artist who paints, makes music-box dioramas, and creates jewelry. The couple recently pooled their talents to create a play, written by Erik and acted out by his marionettes on a set designed and styled by Jessica. The interior design of their apartment is similarly a result of the couple's collaborative efforts: a harmonious coming together of their individual tastes, which culminates in a single vision.

Your home has this harmonious aesthetic. Was one of you responsible for creating the look, or did it develop through a process of give and take? ✳ ERIK: Our contributions are fairly equal. We both collected before we met, and the two aesthetics kind of bleed into one another now. Jesse brought in smaller, more feminine things. ✳ JESSICA: Like the taxidermy birds? (Laughs.) It's definitely a collaboration. And it's a work in progress. For me, the house is like my artwork—like this giant diorama. We're constantly redesigning little areas of it, creating different moods and feelings.

So you see your home as something you'll always be working on, not something that you'll be done with one day? ✳ ERIK: There is no "done." Our aesthetics are constantly evolving. It's nice to be surrounded by things that inspire you, and it's hard to be inspired by the same thing for a long period of time. ✳ JESSICA: We have a friend who has a rule: if she doesn't look at or appreciate something for six months, she gets rid of it. She feels that if you don't love something anymore, you should replace it with something you do love.

When you walk into your home, how do you feel? ✳ JESSICA: We're always really excited when we come home. Erik is on tour a lot, and every time he comes home he says, "God, this is a really nice place." It's just so beautiful and so magical. ✳ ERIK: It's like a little sanctuary. ✳ JESSICA: Yeah, it feels really special to live here. I feel lucky to live here.

Would you ever move out of this space? ✳ ERIK: Apartments are like blank canvases. There's nothing particularly special about the space: it's the stuff in the space that is special to us. ✳ JESSICA: Well, except that we are on the river... ✳ ERIK: We do have some beautiful light, and beautiful views.

You both make art in this space at times. What is it like working together here? ✳ ERIK: That is definitely something that we've had to learn how to do. Jesse was used to working on her own and finds me to be a distraction. ✳ JESSICA: You're so fun! If you're around I want to talk to you and hang out with you. But we can work together. If we have a show coming up, we can work side by side. ✳ ERIK: I can work in a hurricane.

How does working in such close proximity influence your work? ✳ ERIK: Jesse keeps me straight—keeps me true to what I'm supposed to be doing. If I get lazy or a little cavalier about something, she calls me on it, which I really am grateful for. ✳ JESSICA: If he tries to fake something with the puppets—like if the shoes aren't completely handmade—I say, "What's up with the shoes? Aren't you going to put leather and laces on them?" And then, basically, none of my artwork passes out of the house without Erik giving it his stamp of approval. If he doesn't like it, then I don't like it. We have a very similar eye. He's basically an objective version of me. ✳ ERIK: When you are tied up in something of your own creation, it's difficult to be objective. Having someone who is one step away from it makes all the difference. Jesse has given me the best ideas, which I am always quick to acknowledge.

What is your favorite part of the apartment? ✳ ERIK: I like the area in our kitchen where the couch is. It's not a real couch, just this metal thing with cushions. It's the only place that is soft to lie on—that, and the bed. ✳ JESSICA: I like it there too. The light is really amazing. You're surrounded by plants and beautiful views down Warren Street. And that's where our relationship started: we would sit there every night, drinking beer and having these really long conversations. It definitely feels like the part of the house where we come together.

Your bedroom is a striking color. How did you pick that red? ✳ ERIK: I had been looking for that red for our bedroom for a long time. It's the color of dried rose petals. We had things in there that were made of shiny metal and old dark wood, and some things that were a dusty canvas color. It just seemed to be the right color to add. ✳ JESSICA: The color doesn't make us angry, if that's what you were thinking. ✳ ERIK: The color is cool and darkish, almost like leather. Being in that room is like being in the womb, or like sleeping in a giant liver.

I HAD BEEN LOOKING FOR THAT RED

for our bedroom for a long time.

IT'S THE COLOR OF DRIED ROSE PETALS....

Being in that room is like being in the womb, or like

SLEEPING IN A GIANT LIVER.

—ERIK SANKO

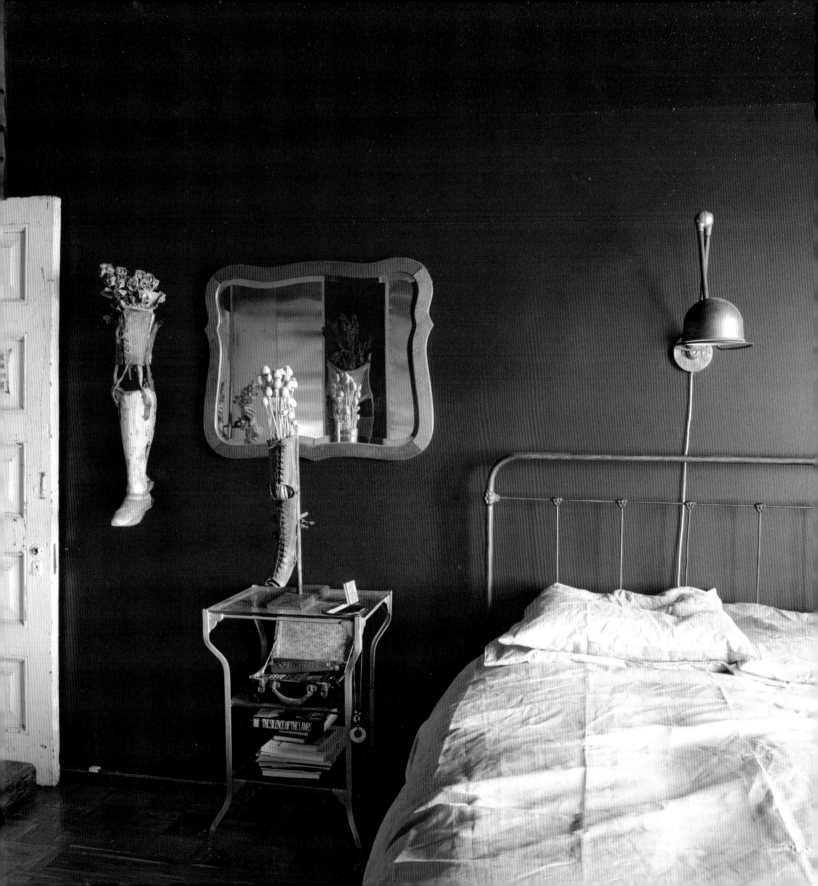

Why do you collect taxidermy? ✳ JESSICA: A lot of people ask us this. I am obsessed with animals and feel really connected to them: oddly, more to the image of animals than to the actual living animals. There is something about the shape and form of animals that I find fascinating and inspiring. ✳ We collect Victorian taxidermy. Back then, you actually had to make an armature for the animals, so each is one of a kind. They were stuffed with wire forms and hay. I have one bird—to make the shape of its head, they wound a ball of thread: it would take three hours to wind a ball that big. I love the time and attention that other people put into preserving the shape of the animal. I love the idea of them being frozen and with us forever.

Was making this place your home a lot of work for you? ✳ ERIK: We don't think of creating our house as work. I feel like it's a guilty pleasure. We surround ourselves with the things that we love.

What is the driving force behind making your home something that is your own? ✳ JESSICA: It's like we were preprogrammed, like birds making their nests. We were just born knowing that we have to get the twigs and bring them to the tree and add the mud. We just have to do it. And doing it makes us joyful. Here, we're in our natural habitat.

What are the reactions that you get from people when they come to your home? ✳ JESSICA: I think people are generally delighted, or curious. ✳ ERIK: It depends on the person. The apartment is a good barometer of what people are like. For our friends, our home is just an extension of us. But this one guy came over, and he walked around, and he didn't say anything… ✳ JESSICA: Even if you don't like it, there are still things you could ask, or say… ✳ ERIK: Yeah, like, "You got a lot of crap!" ∎

I LOVE THE TIME AND ATTENTION

that other people put into

preserving the shape of the animal.

I LOVE THE IDEA OF THEM BEING FROZEN

and with us forever.

—JESSICA GRINDSTAFF

Grandma Prisbrey's Bottle Village

SIMI VALLEY, CALIFORNIA

During her ninety-two-year life, Grandma Prisbrey (1896–1988) was married twice and bore seven children. She began building Bottle Village when, in her sixties, she needed a wind break on her dusty Simi Valley land. Looking for inexpensive materials, she decided on glass bottles after visiting the local dump and finding an abundance of them. She returned to the dump weekly, and Bottle Village eventually grew to encompass thirteen houses and twenty-two sculptures. Prisbrey's creative efforts attracted many visitors, and a few years before her death, some devoted friends founded the Bottle Village Committee to help accommodate them. Today this group preserves Bottle Village (a designated county, state, and national landmark) and provides tours by appointment. Below, Joanne Johnson, a volunteer at the village for thirty years, shares her memories of Grandma Prisbrey and talks about what it takes to preserve her legacy.

Tell me about the first time you came to Bottle Village. How did it make you feel? ✴ I was driving down a street, looking for a store. I was totally new to the neighborhood and was a bit lost, and I ran into Bottle Village by accident. Well, I never did go to the store that day. ✴ It was that magical feeling of finding something that you weren't looking for. It was an excited feeling, like "Oh, wow." And it also felt like going home, if that makes any sense: it was like my mother's attic, my grandmother's bedroom, my dad's basement. There was just all this stuff to look at—all this good stuff. ✴ I began to go to Bottle Village more to visit Grandma Prisbrey than just to look at the place. I liked her, and I would stop by for visits on my way home from work. I realize now that I never talked to her about her art: the visits were completely personal. "How are you feeling?" "Did you go out with your sister today?" That's the kind of relationship we had, and I still have a very personal connection to the place.

The public was always welcome at Grandma Prisbrey's home. In continuing to allow people to see it, are you trying to continue that tradition? ✳ While Grandma was building her Bottle Village, people stopped by, curious about what she was doing. She liked what she called "visiting." A friendly Midwesterner by nature, she loved chatting about her latest creation. As more people came, amazed at her ingenuity, she found her passion. In a lightbulb moment, she realized that tours could bring in some extra money, which she needed in her old age, and she could still have fun "visiting." Bottle Village represents the evolution of an artist, from doing practical home improvements using unconventional materials to this explosion of creativity and joy in entertaining people. Preserving what remains of Bottle Village and keeping it open to the public is our mission, though gaining wholehearted support from the city of Simi Valley has been a challenge. The powers that be here think that the new mall, because it looks like Tuscany, is the hot ticket in town.

What was it like to see the state of Bottle Village after the earthquake in 1994? ✳ I was surprised that all of Bottle Village wasn't demolished, because Simi Valley was seriously hit. It was a massive cleanup. When I see the ruins of the structures, I can remember how everything used to look, and it makes me feel very sad. But the people that see it now still say, "Wow, it's so amazing that she did all of this. There's so much to see!" They are so thrilled, even with what is here now.

41 | BOTTLE VILLAGE

Practically everything I have in this place

SOMEONE HAS GIVEN TO ME,

or I have found.

I FOUND SO MANY DOLLS...

that I didn't know what to do with them.

The natural thing

WAS TO BUILD THEM A HOUSE.

—GRANDMA PRISBREY

What do you think Bottle Village teaches us? ✳ It teaches us so much about human nature and about ourselves: the instinct to create, having a passion for life, enjoying other people, determination, optimism, fearlessness, the absolute necessity of keeping the joy and whimsy of a child close to your heart. Grandma had a difficult life, and no matter what, she kept on going.

House tours today often showcase the homes of great architects, like Frank Lloyd Wright for example. How do you think Grandma Prisbrey's home and her achievements compare to those of others? ✳ Hers is possibly an even greater achievement, considering Grandma had no formal training. Her "architecture school" was mainly on-the-job training. Her masonry skills were remarkable, considering the unforgiving nature of a material such as cement.

What do you think propelled her to create a whole bottle village on her property? ✳ A one-third-acre plot of bone-dry, boring, brown, dusty dirt in Simi Valley was a blank canvas waiting for a vision! First, she built the thirty-foot-long Bottle Wall, which acted as a wind break. Simi is very windy, and there was a poultry farm next-door, so keeping the feathers away was important. Then she built the Pencil House for her collection of seventeen thousand pencils. Instead of a plain cement patio, she created the Mosaic Walkway, embedding thousands of castaway items that she found at the local dump. She was excited about what she was doing, and her ideas just grew. I can easily imagine her lying in bed at night, thinking and planning.

A LADY SAID TO ME,

"What you couldn't do with a million dollars!"

I SAID, "ANYONE CAN DO ANYTHING

with a million dollars—look at Walt Disney.

BUT IT TAKES MORE THAN MONEY

to make something out of nothing,

AND LOOK AT WHAT FUN

I have doing it."

—GRANDMA PRISBREY

Do you think it would be possible to build a place like Bottle Village now? ✳ Simi Valley was a collection of farms and vacant fields back then. Today, it's suburbia; we live by our lawns now. You could never build a place like Bottle Village on a vacant lot here. You would have the city down your throat, if not your neighbors. Bottle Village used to stand out like a billboard, but now it's incrusted in suburbia, which makes its presence even more amazing.

Do you think that Grandma Prisbrey saw building Bottle Village as hard work? ✳ She knew it was hard work, and fun! Most people equate hard work with drudgery: for Grandma, it was an adventure. That to me is the secret of life. You find something that you love to do, and it keeps you vibrant.

Going to her home was very much like going to a performance. She would sing for you and take you on a tour and show you all of her found objects. Has it been very hard to fill her shoes? ✳ Our visitors love to hear Grandma's stories. By keeping it personal, Bottle Village is humanized, and the connection between the viewer, the art, and the artist is preserved. Grandma loved being a performer, and I do too! (Laughs.)

Do you feel her presence when you're here now? ✳ I don't want to say I've seen her ghost… (Laughs.) But there is a feeling I get when I'm here. When I start a tour, I get so filled with energy, and I can close my eyes and see her walking around. My five-year-old granddaughter thinks that Bottle Village is mine, and the funny thing is that when I first started coming to Bottle Village I was thirty, and I looked like a kid, relatively speaking, and people asked me if I was Grandma's granddaughter. Fast-forward twenty years, and people would ask me, "Are you Grandma Prisbrey's daughter?" And now, people ask me, "Are you Grandma Prisbrey?" Time goes by so fast.

Does Grandma Prisbrey's strong character inspire you? ✴ Whenever I feel sorry for myself, I think of Grandma, living by herself, having had all those kids and experiencing the tragedy of all of them dying, even though they were adults, before she did. She's such an inspiration. Once you get out of yourself and turn your energy outward, it's such a better life. She started building Bottle Village when she was sixty. I can't even imagine that.

What has been your favorite part of preserving the village? ✴ Travelers from faraway places come here on a quest to see the Muse of Simi Valley. They leave inspired and enchanted, as if they've seen one important destination on their journey of life. For me, to be a part of that is quite amazing. And it's so much fun to talk to the people. Each one has their own story, and I love finding out about their lives.

What do people remark on the most when they tour the village? ✴ They always say, "How did she do this all by herself?" They remark on seeing the light shine through the bottles, seeing something in the Mosaic Walkway or on a shelf that triggers a memory. They say, "My mother had one of those," or, "I had one of those when I was a kid!"

What do you enjoy most when visiting Bottle Village? ✴ Every time I come here, I see something new. Before, when there weren't so many tall trees and that double-story complex wasn't there, the afternoon sun would come into the round house. The light through the bottles was so thick and golden you felt like you could slice it. I also really like the noise the bottles make in the wind—not when it's really windy, but just when we get those funny little winds that make the leaves swirl around like mini tornados. It's my happy place. I like to participate in life and not just be an observer, and Bottle Village keeps me participating. ■

Mija Bankava's SoHo Loft

Mija Bankava is a painter who has lived in SoHo long enough to have witnessed the transformation of this New York City neighborhood from an artist's mecca in the 1970s to the shopper's mecca that it is today. The iron-clad warehouse building that houses her studio and home, along with those of other artists, is one of a vanishing breed. Her home is filled with her work, which doesn't stop at her paintings but also includes all of the pieces of furniture that she has painted or reupholstered herself. Inside her light-filled loft, Bankava uses color and form to achieve balance and harmony, just as she does on her carefully composed canvases.

Your home has an abundance of space. What does it feel like to live and paint in a space like this? ✳ Well, to me it doesn't even feel like a lot of space. I have always needed a lot of room for expansion. Picasso loved to have multiple houses: he would fill up one space with his work, and then just close the door and move on to create the next space. If I could, I would do that. ✳ I feel that my house is a work in progress, and I wish there were more chances to expand. I constantly have new ideas, new sets of furniture, new compositions.

All this sunlight must make the plants very happy. ✳ I don't know if my plants are happy; I hope so. Plants are an integral part of my surroundings, but to me they are more about shapes and forms. I really don't like normal looking plants. They have to have character. They have to take on some bizarre form. I like having special pots and

pedestals for them. To me, they're visual elements. ✳ And I think light is very important, too: how it changes the colors. I used to watch the sun a lot. I think it's precious.

What influences your color palette? ✳ My color choices come from instinct, from things
that I'm drawn to. I tend to wear black most of the time, but when it comes to things
around me, I like a lot of color. ✳ You have to feel what is right with color: what
balances out other things, how one shape looks against another shape. It's all in the
same realm as painting. You have to have areas that are quiet against very busy ones.
Working with pattern, especially, you have to have a sense for color, because it can all
become so overwhelming.

Do you have a favorite spot in the house? ✳ It's hard to say what my favorite area is. I've
created all these different areas, and I love to change things and bring new energies to
things and allow for other types of stimulation.

How do you feel when you come home and close the door behind you? ✳ My home is a
refuge, especially in this neighborhood, which is very intense and populated. When I
get home I can't even believe that I am in the city. It is very quiet here. ✳ I love coming back here when I've been away, because I feel like I can reinvent something or add
some new thing or try out a new idea of how I want to work here. Wherever I go, I
am redecorating things in my head. If I sense imbalance in a space, it's like a part of
my body has been put in an uncomfortable position. If I had to live in a place—like a
furnished apartment—where I couldn't change anything, I would go slightly crazy.
There is very rarely a time when I can actually live happily with what's around me,
without being able to make it my own. It's awful, actually, to be this way, because

you become super-critical and very unaccepting. (Laughs.) If I visit someone's home, I can't help but to start redecorating it in my head. I would never say anything, of course…

Have you ever considered decorating anyone else's home? ✳ I've had friends over the years ask me to come and help them decorate, and I won't have any of it. When you let others make decisions for you, everything starts to look the same. ✳ The whole idea of "decorating"…Well, I wouldn't want to do it. I don't care what your taste is, it's yours; it's an extension of your personality. I hate the idea of somebody else coming into a person's home and changing it. Then you don't know who the person is anymore.

How do people react when they come into your home? ✳ Well, it varies. Some people are uncomfortable with it. If you really put your personality into creating your home, why should others feel comfortable with it? I had one man remark on how practical the shelving in my kitchen was, of all things. I didn't know how to react to that. Practicality doesn't come into play. My things are objects that make up compositions in space. Some of my couches aren't even functional; I just like to play with them as shapes and forms. ✳ Men have the strongest reactions, maybe because women—or at least my women friends—are accustomed to personalizing their homes, and what I am doing is more natural to them. One time I had a party, and I noticed that all the women were gathered together around the kitchen table talking. All the men were sitting in my red bedroom. When I asked the men what they were doing, they all said they just really liked being in there. I guess men like red bedrooms. ✳ Men generally say that they feel as though they're in a different place when they come here—a place not of this world.

My things are objects that make up

COMPOSITIONS IN SPACE.

Some of my couches aren't even functional;

I JUST LIKE TO PLAY

with them as shapes and forms.

—MIJA BANKAVA

Would you say that creating your home has been a lot of work? ✳ To me, creating my home has not been work: I do not see it that way. When I got the other side of my loft back from the renters and had to redo the walls, I was so happy. I actually wish I could change more things; although, once you get a certain balance, you can't move anything.

What has been your driving force in creating your space? ✳ People live in different parts of themselves, and as far as I'm concerned, my house is an extension of my paintings—an extension of my visual world. I can't imagine working in a white box with nothing but my paintings to look at. I have to bring everything—every curious object imaginable—into my studio and be visually stimulated by it. It's not that I like clutter: everything has to be in its proper place. Coming back from flea markets in the country, I run to my studio with all the things I've bought and immediately start arranging the new things with the old. Creating a composition is what it is, again and again, in my surroundings and in my paintings. ◼

I hate the idea of somebody else

COMING INTO A PERSON'S HOME

and changing it. Then you don't know who

THE PERSON IS ANYMORE.

—MIJA BANKAVA

Main Delay, Peter Rittmaster's Summerhouse

MAINE

Peter Rittmaster—an artist, designer, and inventor—has vacationed in Maine since his early childhood. Today, he and his companion, Laurie Mallet, reside in New York City but spend a good part of each summer at his family's vacation house, where they enjoy a simple life without pretense. Poised alongside a lake on one-and-a-half wooded acres, the house accommodates a steady stream of guests throughout the season. A totem pole stationed at the dock announces the primary point of arrival, and other objects, like a teepee and a dummy in a rowboat, eternally fishing on the lake, signal that this is a playful place meant for amusement and relaxation.

How long have you been coming to the house? ✳ I have been coming to this part of Maine for more than fifty years; first, as a kid, to go to summer camp. My mother and father would come to visit me. They always stayed at the same inn, and that became their place. Eventually, when a property became available nearby, they decided to buy it, and my father and I built the house there together five years later. ✳ It was our seasonal house. Seasonal houses are not very common anymore: what you see now are million-dollar year-round homes, or second homes. That's sad, because summerhouses are a wonderful thing. ✳ It's great coming to the house at the beginning of every summer, greeting it and opening it up, and then, at the end of the season, closing it up until next year. When you leave, you know that you won't see the house for another six months, so you thank the house for all the great experiences it has given you.

How does the house make you feel when you come to it every summer? ✳ We want the house to be a place that makes you smile when you're here. When I first get here it's sad. Everything is covered up: there are mothballs scattered around. It's time to check in with the house. I spend a week fixing little things here and there, bringing the house back to life. You have to make the house happy first, because then it will make you happy. I once had a friend who would tell me that his house hated him, and I told him that he'd have to listen to his house and see what it needed. Seems he's since made up with his house, because he doesn't tell me that it hates him anymore. (Laughs.)

What kind of activities do you enjoy with your guests? ✳ When I first started entertaining with Laurie, she'd say, "How are we going to manage with all of these guests?" and I'd say, "By not entertaining them! We'll all entertain each other." ✳ We have many guests that come every year. Just this past year we had sixty or so. They enjoy all kinds of activities, like cooking their own breakfast out of doors each morning, having drinks and hors d'oeuvres on the dock in the evening, eating dessert around a fire in the tee-pee. The teepee is one of the greatest inventions: there isn't any other structure that you can have a fire going in for as long as you want, without having a chimney. Our new one is twenty-five feet in diameter. Putting it up every year is an activity in and of itself. Traditionally, it was the Sioux women who would put up the teepees. The woman with the straightest poles on her teepee was considered to be a prized house-wife. The men in my family try to make the Sioux women proud each year. The house itself sits on an old Native American preservation. Serious thought was put into its orientation on the land to take advantage of the light and views. ✳ All these things make it a very special place, and when we're here, we're filled with this good feeling.

Do you have any rules for your guests? ✳ All of our guests are free to do whatever they want. We encourage people to look through all of the drawers in the kitchen and get to know where everything is. They can use anything they want to, as long as they put it back where they found it. We make a mockery of the kitchen by doing the bulk of the cooking outside. We have at least twelve cast-iron skillets that our guests use to cook their own eggs outside over an open fire. It's one of the experiences they say they miss the most after they leave. ✳ We like to do a lot of things outside. The house itself is quite small. We have constant yard sale competitions, where we set out in different directions not knowing where the yard sales are, and then we come back and see who found the most interesting thing. The guests love this game.

Tell me a little bit about the decor of the house? ✳ There are definitely things that make you laugh. We don't take the house too seriously. It's constantly changing. We have these cabinets of curiosity in all of the rooms now, and we keep adding things to them. When you're walking on the beach or through the woods and you pick up an object that you think is really fabulous, you take it back to the house and it becomes part of a cabinet. Then our guests change the objects around, so the cabinets are constantly changing. Then we have artist friends who find an object around the house and transform it into a piece of art. Then there are the "house presents" that our guests bring us. Somehow it's always the most ridiculous and bizarre thing that they think will look great here. Every year we get crazier things, many of which I end up transforming into art objects.

I once had a friend who would

TELL ME THAT HIS HOUSE HATED HIM,

and I told him that he'd

HAVE TO LISTEN TO HIS HOUSE

and see what it needed.

—PETER RITTMASTER

Tell me about the totem poles. ✳ The totem pole off the dock is an original Northwest Coast Salish pole. It's been there since we built the house forty years ago. The two at the entrance to the house are ones I carved. They came later. I had a fly-fishing friend who worked for Central Maine Power, and he told me they were taking down some transmission lines. The poles were Western red cedar, a hundred and ten years old—sixty years old to begin with, and in the ground for fifty years. He asked me, "Would you like to get a couple?" I said, "Geez, I'd love to!" Red cedar is a traditional material used to make totem poles. ✳ So I made a couple of cradles, sketched on the poles with charcoal, and started carving. My friend said, "Aren't you going to practice first?" And I said, "Absolutely not!" I had used a chain saw for most of my life. Once I got them finished, I decided to use them as supports for a rain canopy. I found an old wooden canoe to put up there, and we had a party to put up the poles. Many of our neighbors came out from around the lake and we had a barbeque. The men were trying to get these seventeen-foot poles up, and we're all pushing and pulling. And the women are watching this, and they're relegated to the chore of preparing us lunch, and some are starting to get indignant. Finally one of them gets very vocal about it and said, "What's going on here? What kind of 'erection' party is this?" And I said, "Oh my God. Of course, any ladies that would like to take part in the 'erection' party are welcome!" (Laughs.) Anyway, it was a delightful afternoon. And that's the lore of the poles.

Tell me about Harry the Fisherman? ✳ My stepson and I were walking in New York City one day, and in a dumpster, we saw a CPR dummy. We couldn't just leave it there, so we took it back to Maine. It sat there for weeks, and then my friend and I found a boat at the dump and decided to put the dummy in it. We dressed it up, and it became Harry the Eternal Fisherman. He's out there in the lake, fishing every day. He's a great game

warden decoy: when the wardens come out they try to give him a ticket, because he doesn't have a fishing license. That keeps the wardens busy. He's been out there for ten years now. We change his clothes every year, and everyone comes by and says hello to him.

How are you and your guests different when you get to the house? ✳ This past summer we had a guest who asked me if I had a fast wireless connection. I told him that I just had dial-up but that he could take the boat out to the local library and use the internet there for free. He thought I was crazy to suggest such a thing, but there he was, taking a nice boat ride to the library and back. Now our guests can pick up a wireless connection right here, but at least they're still checking their email on a dock overlooking a beautiful lake!

Do you want your guests to come away with anything in particular? ✳ We have this magic of being alone with people here, of being able to talk with them and interact with them in a way that we can't in our regular, busy lives in the city. We have guests who come every year who say, "How can we live more like this?" Really, it doesn't take a great deal of money: if you choose to live this way, that's enough. Things are cheaper in the country. Everything isn't as readily available, but you learn to live with what's near at hand, and that's really great.

Tell me about the name "Main Delay." ✳ My mother gave the house that name years ago. It's a *jeu de mots* on the city of Mandalay—a place my mother loved very much—but it's also what the house is really about, this delayed, laid-back place where we keep the world at bay. Life is easy here, with no need to rush or run here and there. It's a place where we don't take ourselves too seriously, and where we enjoy the luxury of time. ■

WE HAVE THIS MAGIC OF BEING ALONE

with people here, of being able to

TALK WITH THEM AND INTERACT WITH THEM

in a way that we can't in our regular,

BUSY LIVES IN THE CITY.

—PETER RITTMASTER

St. Elmo Village, Roderick Sykes & Jacqueline Alexander-Sykes's home

LOS ANGELES

In the mid-1960s, Roderick Sykes rented a few bungalows on St. Elmo Drive, in an inner-city neighborhood of Los Angeles, with his uncle Rozzell Sykes. Both men were artists, and in 1969, they founded St. Elmo Village there as a local arts cooperative. When the bungalows' owner wanted to tear down the buildings to make room for an apartment complex, they joined forces with other artists to purchase the properties. Following Rozzell's death in 1994, Roderick, a photographer and mixed-media artist, became the director of St. Elmo Village. Today, he runs the non-profit organization with his wife, the painter and photographer Jacqueline Alexander-Sykes. Together they maintain the cluster of small buildings and host art classes where young and old, experienced and novice, come to participate in a variety of creative activities.

The outside of St. Elmo Village is so inviting. Was that intentional, or did it just happen? ✳ Los Angeles is not known for people saying "hello." Folks just don't speak to each other. So our intent was to create something—we didn't know what exactly, at first—that would make our neighbors ask, "What are you doing? What's going on?" We would then get the opportunity to meet.

What are some of the ways that the village has influenced the neighborhood? ✳ We have children that are into their art. We have parents that are recognizing the creativity of

their children: not just putting their art on the refrigerator but framing it and hanging it on the wall. Any time you have a place that recognizes people as human beings first, it affects so many things, like the crime level, for example. We don't have bars on the windows in the neighborhood anymore. This place is a sanctuary, and a sea of inspiration for what people can do, in their own yards and in their own lives. People are now saying, "This is my neighborhood, my community. I live here. I care about this place, so I am going to show that I care." ✶ The village is an example of doing what you love and loving what you do. I read something by Kahlil Gibran that said, "Work is love made visible." That hit the nail right on the head. And when people come together to build something—learning from each other, discovering together—they take ownership of it. The village becomes their second home.

Do you see yourself being at the village forever? ✶ It's hard for me to leave! I have a '93 Dodge Caravan that I drive, and it has 27,000 miles on it. It's very difficult to get me out of here, man, because I love it. I love the effect it has on me. I love seeing how it affects others as they walk though here, seeing what they discover. Many people have dreamed about creating such a place, and it becomes an inspiration for them. The village has grown to the point where folks from all over the globe come through here.

What can you tell me about the outdoor decor? ✶ When I'm not here, I still want to meet you. So I create these things that talk to you and say who I am when I'm not physically present. ✶ We've had all kinds of plants over the years, but having annuals was too much work. I want it to look good. I don't just want to do it halfway. So I had to figure out what kind of plants I could put in that were low maintenance. Succulents and cacti were ideal, and they can stand up to all kinds of abuse. I haven't forgotten that I used to sword fight with plants as a kid. You have to remember; you can't forget.

What about the unlikely planters, like the painted toilet bowls? ✴ Well, we needed planters, and all my life my grandmother used to take my grandfather's old boots, when he got holes in them, and she would paint them and put dirt in them and grow stuff out of them. Actually, she'd use anything that would hold dirt. So we had all this junk around—toilets, old barbeque pits, bathtubs—and we didn't have money to go buy planters, so we painted the junk and we used it. It wasn't a plan to have this stuff. It was like, "What can we do with it?"

Tell me about the murals? ✴ We came home one night, and they had just put in new streetlights, and we saw our shadows on the ground and we started tracing them and painting them in. We just wanted to make the village more beautiful, and we saw the cement as this large canvas. ✴ We usually painted murals on large boards, but one day we didn't have any boards, so we started painting on the cement, and that turned into a much bigger project, which was so much fun for everyone. We did it all in a week— all 10,000 square feet. It was some love affair, boy. We worked day and night. We were on the ground fightin' for space. You had to hurry and claim your spot before there wasn't any space left.

How did the pond come about? ✳ It was a really hot summer, and we had the Summer Youth Kids here. This was their first job, workin' in the village clearing away this three-by-five-foot shed that used to be a paint studio. So they kung-foo chopped it and karate kicked it and took it down. We decided to make a pond, so we took trips to the Ferndale Mountains and gathered stones, and we brought back sand from Santa Monica beach to mix with the mortar. We went to all the beaches and all the mountains in the area. We used coat hangers to make wire frames to hold the cement together and bags from the dry cleaners to seal it. ✳ The kids were really into it. The majority of them were between five and twelve, about thirty of them altogether, and they worked for a year. They would come early in the morning, and I'd have to make them go home at night. My thing with them was that you work with rhythm: when you mix the water and the sand, you create music. And they had this music happening. The difference between work and play is attitude. ✳ The mural alongside the pond came later, but the same kids that built the pond painted it. Now they are old men and women, but their pieces are still here, and they come back with their kids and visit and chill out.

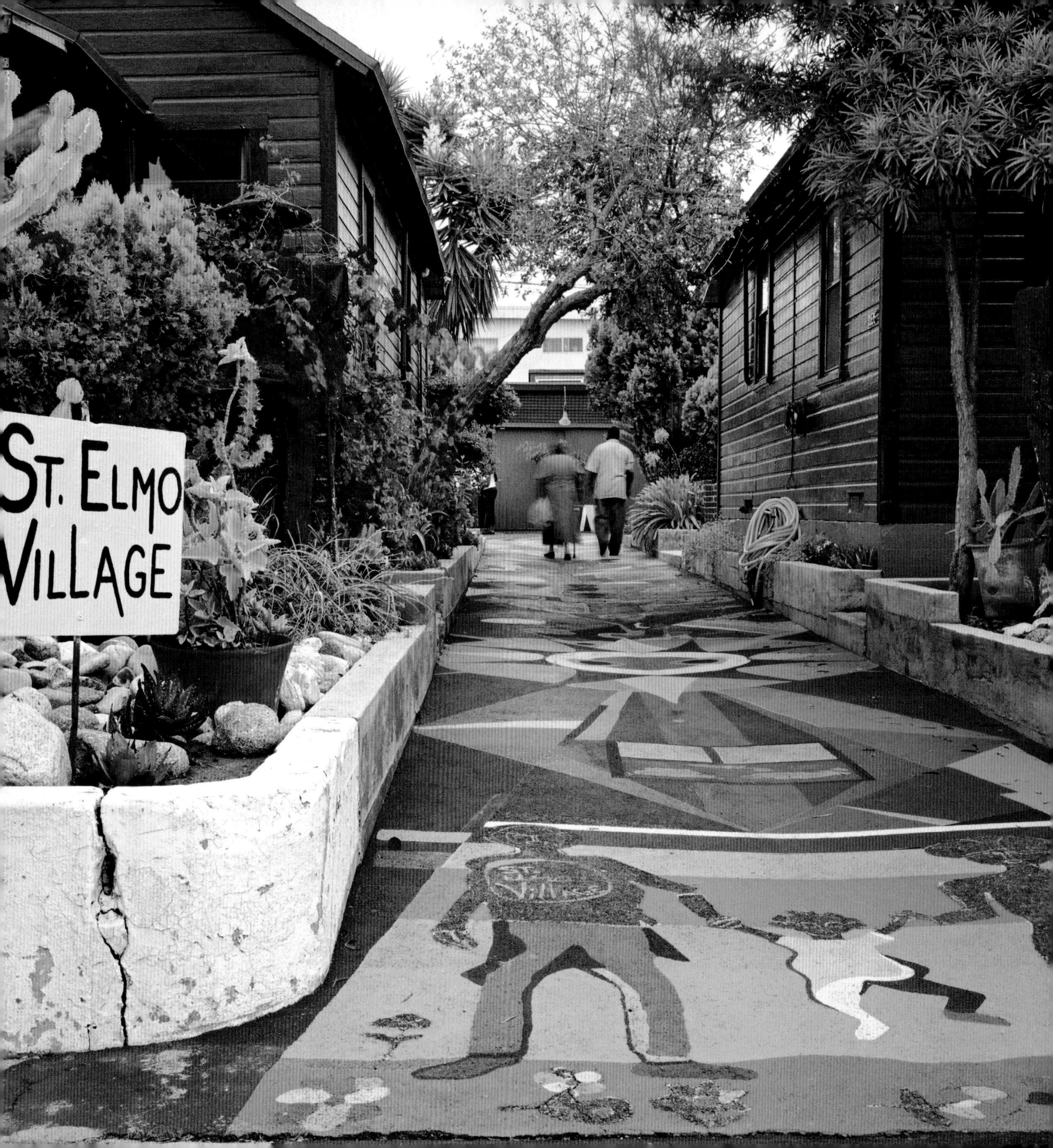
ST. ELMO
VILLAGE

Tell me about the photographs on your walls. ✳ These are the people that I've been fortunate enough to meet and that are part of my life. I know every last one of them. ✳ People have been positive about my photography, and when you wake up in the morning and see something that you've done, that just gives you an injection. When I walk out of my door, wherever I look, I see something that inspires me. Your creativity feeds your spirit, and you know you can do something more. And I never thought I could do very much that was worthwhile. (Laughs.) I was, as they say, "least likely to succeed." My art teacher told me, "Forget art. Get a good job!" Now people say to me, "Why aren't you making art to sell in galleries? Instead, you're here pulling weeds, sweeping the streets?" Well, this is our art. It's not separate from life: it's living as art. The village is about the process of creating, about what it takes to create. ■

WHEN I WALK OUT OF MY DOOR,

wherever I look, I see

SOMETHING THAT INSPIRES ME.

—RODERICK SYKES

TAMI LEE'S GREENPOINT APARTMENT

BROOKLYN, NEW YORK

This apartment no longer exists in real time. In 2003, after living there for three years, Tami Lee was pushed out by her landlord. Newly married, she currently lives with her architect husband (and their dog, Demon) in another apartment in Brooklyn. While the couple's new home is remarkable for its expansive, minimalist design, Tami's old apartment traded on the strength of individual objects, layered one on top of the other. It was a place where she indulged all of her creative urges. Today Tami derives most of her creative fulfillment from her work, as the New York District visual merchandiser for the retail store Anthropologie. There she continues to create show-stopping layered environments for all to enjoy.

———

How did you choose the objects and colors that characterized your apartment? ✳ I think, overall, I just became obsessed with collecting things. Not necessarily things that would create a full collection of like items, but things that would collaborate well with each other. I was one of those kids who always went to flea markets and got stuff, and I had such a hard time getting rid of anything, ever, that it just kept building. I wanted to create an apartment around all the stuff. The whole apartment was basically layers and layers of stuff. I like deep, earthy tones, and they created a nice backdrop for it all.

Did you ever feel hindered by the size of some of the objects that you wanted to purchase for your apartment? Some of them—like the stuffed bear in your living room—are very large. ✳ I saw the stuffed bear and immediately said, "I have to have it." Surprisingly, it fit into the cab, lying across my lap. I basically had to hug it to carry it into the apartment, and everyone on the street was staring at me. I think that with everything I collected there was always that moment when I said to myself, "I have to have it."

Do you see your place as having a death theme? Did you intentionally create such a theme for the apartment? ✳ My apartment came across as a little macabre in areas, but that definitely wasn't my mindset. Everything I had kind of had a soul to me. I never wanted to part with things, and that probably had to do with the loss I experienced when my mother died. But the taxidermy, for example, isn't about a dead creature: it's more about how I love that the animal is captured in its form and it's like a life that never leaves, because it's always there. ✳ I think the coffin was about me seeing it and thinking, "Wow! I can't believe there is a coffin here," and feeling like I had to have it, and then finding a mannequin that fit inside of it. It's just part of a process by which I would find ways of combining the things I had in interesting ways.

Did you have an area in the apartment that you were particularly content to be in? ✳ I spent most of my time in the living room. It was very cozy and had the right amount of stuff. I think that in the bedroom I went a little overboard, and it wasn't the most relaxing environment to sleep in. There was too much happening in there visually.

Did you get to a point where you felt like you had too much stuff? ✳ I never edited things out: it was always about adding. But once I started to edit, I couldn't stop. Once one thing was gone, then the other thing didn't work and that had to go. It was like moving in reverse.

What was it like knowing that you would have to move? How did that affect the look of your apartment? ✳ I knew I would be the last tenant before the place was fully renovated, so I didn't feel like I had any boundaries. I just went overboard there. It was a lot of work for a temporary place, but I saw it as my chance to go all out. ✳ It all goes back to when I was growing up. My parents would always let me do whatever I wanted to my bedroom. Every couple of years, my room would change. I would repaint it, rearrange it: it was constantly changing.

What do you miss most about that apartment, now that you have left it? ✳ I miss how comforting it was. The way I live now is, honestly, more comfortable, because I feel like my entire life has cleaned up since I cleaned up my living space. I feel like a much more organized person now. But my old apartment was a place where I felt very content living alone. I don't think that if I had lived alone in a simpler place I would have felt as comfortable. Being surrounded by stuff that had some meaning to me felt very comforting.

THERE WAS NO THOUGHT PROCESS

of "I have no room for that." It was,

"I HAVE TO HAVE IT, AND THEN

I'll figure out where it's going to go."

—TAMI LEE

Did you end up donating a lot of things, or selling things, when you moved to your new place? ✳ I did a flea market in Chelsea for a weekend and sold a lot of stuff. I gave a lot away, and I threw a lot out. Some stuff made it to my current apartment, but 80 percent of what I had before I moved is gone. It's amazing, I just realized how little meaning all of these things that I thought had so much meaning really had. My old apartment was almost like part of my outfit, part of who I was and how I put things together. It's still a part of me, that feeling of who I was. Now we refer to it as "Old Tami."

What kind of response did you get to your old place? ✳ A lot of people were just shocked and couldn't believe how much stuff I had. Or they reacted to how dark the apartment was. They would say that it was very cavelike and that it was hard to know what time it was. To me, it was my own personal escape from the everyday. I think I liked blocking out everything else.

Did you see it as a lot of work? ✳ The whole time I lived there I never rearranged: I just added. When I moved in, before I even unpacked, I started picking out colors and wallpaper. I wanted to get the base set, to establish the structure before placing the furniture. The most exciting time for me was when I finished painting and started putting stuff up. Every now and then, late at night or on weekends, I would layer things on. I went to flea markets all the time, and every time I saw something that I wanted I would just figure out a way to work it in. There was no thought process of "I have no room for that." It was, "I have to have it, and then I'll figure out where it's going to go."

What was the feeling you had when you entered your apartment and closed the door behind you? ✳ It definitely felt like home. Five minutes after getting there, I would be in my sweatpants. It felt very cozy there.

Have you ever wanted to buy things that you saw, say, in a furniture catalog? ✳ I like when my place is one of a kind, and when my stuff is one of a kind. I make a lot of my own clothing; things that are one-offs. I like that they are mine. And that's the thrill of going to the flea markets, because generally you find these items that only a few other people have. I like taking something ordinary and turning it into something extraordinary, making something special that is really probably just junk. ■

★ SLICED MEATS ★
Tasty Tempting Ready to Serve

iTH A
HOOK

Lenny Weiner's Apartment,
Peter Cooper Village

NEW YORK CITY

Lenny Weiner has always had a flare for decorating. As far back as he can remember, he has altered the homes in which he and his family lived to make them more beautiful. In his retirement, the union steamfitter and former Golden Gloves welterweight champion finds decorating a way to remain in the present and to connect with the people about whom he cares the most. He plans to live out his days in his current one-bedroom apartment in New York's East Village, which he has made, through trompe l'oeil effects and imagination, into everything he finds ideal in a home.

How long have you lived in your apartment? ✳ I've been here seven years. I started working on things not too long after I retired, and never seriously. Nothing was too serious: everything was always, "I'll do this" and "I'll do that," and then it just got bigger and bigger and developed into something. ✳ Like with that chandelier…I wanted to put something on the ceiling, so I just started with this little circle, and I said, "This will look nice there…and here are these stained glass things that would look nice…and the mirrors…And I think this gold would look nice, and maybe I'll have a star pointing out," and on and on and on.

Will you tell me about the staircase? ✳ Well, I didn't want the typical chair on the side of the fireplace. I know you can't go wrong with it, but I said, "I have to get something different." I always read the magazines that I get sent, and there is this one that advertises all kinds of staircases pretty cheap. That's part of the thing, too: I have to do things on the cheap, because I'm retired. So this iron staircase was $450 stripped, and I didn't know what I was gonna do to it, but then I saw it and I said, "I'll use wooden steps for the treads, and this decorative thing," and then I said, "Maybe I'll put a plant on the steps," and so on and so forth, like that.

What motivates you to do this? ✳ Trying to entertain myself, I would say. I'd never work, like, seven hours straight, but maybe seven different days, for an hour a day. It's something to concentrate on, and something I like to do. Sometimes, if you can get even five or ten minutes of concentration, it's really fun. It tickles me, using your imagination and getting into it. ✳ Then there's the process of going and getting the things. You see what you want in your mind, or on paper. Then you go to the store and see something and say, "Look at this! This is exactly what I'm lookin' for." ✳ So that's the objective: to get it going enough that you can pick at it now and then. I like to do it because it means I got something to think about, something to do, something to keep me moving and interested. To think that it was finished and that I completed it, I probably wouldn't enjoy it anymore.

My philosophy is that if you

HAVE SOMETHING NICE,

you'll always find a spot for it.

IT'S JUST LIKE LEARNING A WORD

and putting it in the back of your mind:

SOMEDAY YOU'LL USE IT.

—LENNY WEINER

Tell me about the parlor area. ✳ That's the first area people look at when they come into the apartment. It really grabs them and takes their breath away. It started when I decided to have my dinner table there, instead of in the kitchen. I liked to look out the window. But I decided that I needed a taller table so I could look down—not just out. Then I said, "If I can just cover the vent here with some grass, I'd get a nice effect." And then I said, "If I can expand it there and put in a tree, I could have what I always wanted to have—a terrace in the parlor!" I cut it off with a divider, and it gives you that feeling you're someplace else. ✳ Then I wanted something better on the ceiling. I really believe in decorating ceilings; otherwise, it's wasted space. Every area has to have some significance—something that somebody would say, "Ooh, I didn't know you could do this." So I said, "Why couldn't I put a mirror on the ceiling?" My next-door neighbor came in to borrow something, and while I was gettin' it, he looks at the ceiling and sees the reflection of the window, and he says, "Gee, I ain't got no window up there!" And I said, "What? You ain't got a window up there?" And I played right along with it. (Laughs.)

Tell me about the little girl who visits you. ✳ I have a little gardener—my neighbor's little girl. She started to pick off the dead leaves on the partition one day, and I said, "Wow, I didn't see those things. Can you do this all the time?" So I give her a pail and a pair of scissors, and she goes around picking off the dead leaves. She crawls on the floor, and I say, "I can never get those!" She's got her own toys on the fountain: that's the only time I put the fountain on, when she comes.

I really believe in

DECORATING CEILINGS;

otherwise, it's wasted space.

Every area has to

HAVE SOME SIGNIFICANCE.

—LENNY WEINER

What can you tell me about the mirrored wall with the New York skyline? ✳ When I was a young kid, my father died: I was, like, nine. I had a Catholic Big Brother, and he sort of helped me out for three, four years, and it was good. So I decided to fill up some of my time by joining the Catholic Big Brothers myself, and I got this kid. Same thing: no father. Nice kid. I'm still very close to the family. We still see each other, especially around the holidays, and birthdays. So, at any rate, as a gift this one Christmas a couple of years ago, they give me these four mirrors that make up part of the New York skyline. So I said, "I have to find a place for them." ✳ My philosophy is that if you have something nice, you'll always find a spot for it. It's just like learning a word and putting it in the back of your mind: someday you'll use it. So I started with the mirrors and expanded with more mirrors and more mirrors and made it into something special, for the family. It was more of a challenge, and it turned out to be a nice piece. ✳ I'm still workin' on it. Like, I got the Twin Towers up there, to show some kind of defiance, or patriotism, and I put halos on the top. But then I decided to scrape off the paint on the underside and have just the outline of the towers, and now it's a lot more symbolic—just like I wanted it. I always know what I want, but I'm not sure how to get it, until I see it and say, "Now that works."

What can you tell me about the wall with the stars and hands over your couch? ✳ This is a special wall. First of all, I don't like a lot of pictures around the house. I never got a feeling for paintings and stuff like that: they just don't give me any good feelings, lookin' at them. So I fiddled with this wall a lot. I believe so much in the sky, in the universe. I enjoy reading about it and about all the philosophies of the hereafter. I hear that everyone who comes out of jail says, "Look at that sky!" So I'm trying to capture something about that on the wall. Do I think I got it? I don't know. It looks interesting. ✳ The hands are to signify the beginning of man. They are like those done by one of those famous artists in the old country—Michelangelo. God touching, giving life to man, that was the vision: of the love, of the heavens. What does this mean, to go to heaven? It means that you have that feeling of love throughout. There is no thinking ahead. There's no thinking in the past. There's just constant good feelings that you have when you are in love, when you feel loved. That is the feeling that we are all trying to get in our lifetime, that we get touches of here and there that we don't even recognize.

Do you enjoy showing your home to people? How do they react? ✳ I get a kick out of it, not that I get a lot of visitors...Most of them have the same reaction. They take a deep breath, like "Wow," they are amazed. Everyone says, "Someone should see this." ✳ It's not a glamorous apartment, and I tell them that if I was married or had a partner I couldn't do this, because I couldn't take the criticism. I know when I'm doing somethin' it may not be right in the beginning, but I'm gonna get it, and if somebody starts judging me and I feel the pressure, I can't handle it: that takes all the creativity away. I know a couple of people who are always criticizing this or that, but still I could see that they drew in their breath...So this tells me that it really is pretty good.

What do you want in a home? ✳ In my house, you can almost tell by lookin' around what I want. I want to have privacy in different areas: outside on the terrace, so-to-speak; in the reading area by the fireplace. I want different areas to enjoy certain kinds of things, so I don't feel cooped up. No doubt, I feel different in my different areas, like I've gone someplace else. I would love to have all these areas be real—real getaways, onto a terrace, into a big reading room. ✳ You can see what I would like in a home, only it's in miniature, because it's the closest I could come! (Laughs.) ■

FINK FARM, LARRY FINK & MARTHA POSNER'S HOME

Larry Fink, a native New Yorker, has been a professional photographer for the past forty-five years. He has published many books and is the recipient of many prestigious grants. His wife Martha, originally from Ohio, is a sculptor and painter whose work is widely exhibited. Their property, affectionately called Fink Farm, is located in the middle of a 250,000-acre forest. It encompasses a main house, a large barn (which houses both of the artists' studios), a small barn (which houses Larry's tractor), and at least four other small houses; in addition, there is a large fenced-in barnyard and various coops that shelter the smaller animals and birds. Larry and Martha relish the physical nature of life on the farm, where they care for more animals and grow more vegetables than can be easily named. Although it's a lot of work, it's the kind of work for which they both live.

When did you first come to the farm? ∗ LARRY: It was 1973. I was married to Joan Snyder, the painter, at the time. She had a desire to be in the country, not me. But I said to myself, and to Joan, "You know, I don't want to do this, but we're married, and it's what you wanna do, so let's go searching." So after three years of searching, we finally came across this place at the end of the road. The place was piled up with buildings and exhibited an appetite for growth, and Snyder liked it for practical reasons, but she feared its massiveness. But I said, "This is the place. There is no other," and so we bought it.

How long did it take you to adjust to the country? ✳ LARRY: About a year and a half. At that time I moved out of the city entirely, and it was then that I really started to like it. ✳ The first year was spent in tears, because of the crippling amount of work we had to do. I had always been the handyman around the loft, but this was more than I had bargained for. I had to learn to prioritize. I also learned that I loved to work with my body. I was always a putterer and a procrastinator, but this took that condition to a passionate, illogical end, which is to say that there is never a moment when I can leave things well enough alone.

Martha, when did you first come to the farm, and what was your first impression? ✳ MARTHA: I first came here in 1990 or '91. Larry was on winter break from Bard, and he invited me out here. One of the first things I saw coming down the road was some rolled-up old fencing. It was all copper and rusted, and it was covered with snow, and I thought, "I want to do a piece about that one day." ✳ The other thing that happened was that Larry took me up one of the hills into the woods, to what we call the Medieval Forest. There is a particular grove of trees that grows there like in Sleeping Beauty's palace. The tree trunks go up ten feet, then literally arch back down to the ground and come up again. They look like huge vines, and their branches have thorns on them. Seeing that really did it for me. Everyone who knows me or my artwork knows I have a lot of pagan in me. It was just unbelievable for me to see this place.

What is it like to experience the seasons at the farm? Do you have favorites? ✳ MARTHA: Spring is always my favorite. There are thousands upon thousands of tulips here—every year, I plant between 750 and 2,000 of them. Every path and all the wooded areas have them, and they produce an explosion of color. ✳ Winter is beautiful too. Sometimes you get these winters where everything is white, and ice crystals cover the trees. Everything looks like glass, like an enchanted forest. When you live in a place like this, you really have to interact with winter; you can't just pull into your covered garage and walk into your house. It's very different to live in winter, rather than hide from winter. * LARRY: I love the winter. I love the cold. Even in my older age, I like the cold wind against my face. I like to fashion myself a hero, and since, in the real world of social interaction, it's very rare that I become one, I cultivate possibilities within this little empire we call home. Winter makes me into a hero. When the big snow falls, I get on my tractor and I get at it, hitting that snow right in the face, any which way I can.

Do you have a "farm story" that you'd like to tell me? * LARRY: When I first got here, I would be alone all winter, and all the farmers—and there were many of them, more than there are now—would take bets on whether or not I was going to last another season. There was this one snow—a wonderful powder snow about a foot and a half deep, but with drifts up to six feet. A drift was blocking our road down below, so here I come in my truck, and the farmers are all watching me secretly from their kitchen windows, and I put the truck in low third and, like an electric razor, or a surfer down the tube, I just sliced right through the drift to the end of the road. I created this wave above my truck about twenty feet in the air, man. The snow was coming in the windows, and I couldn't see a thing. It was like living inside one of Hokusai's waves for a minute and pushing it in front of you and being swallowed by it. It was exquisite! * Needless to say, it was after that little flurry of adventure that I started to gain some respect with the local farmers. (Laughs.)

What are some of your favorite farm tasks? * LARRY: I like the tractor work. I used to love cutting wood. Now that I'm older, I don't take as many chances, though I can still buck a good tree. I don't have as many macho identity issues. It's pretty much just the work of the day. * Over the years, Martha and I have done a lot of things to take care

of this place. It doesn't have the same primitive challenges. I tend to do things when they come about; I sort of think that the day will create its own motion. Martha likes to put motion to the day.

Would you mind listing some of your farm tasks? ✳ MARTHA: Well, I get up and, in the summer, I usually water the potted plants. If it's been dry, I water in the garden. I tend to the weeds. If I'm selling tomatoes to the restaurants, I like to pick them in the morning, when it's cool, and bring them inside. I check on the cats in the various houses and feed them. Then I go to the barn and shovel a bit, and I feed everyone there: the rabbits and the guinea fowl, and the peacocks, and the chickens. Then I feed everyone in the barnyard: the sheep and goats and llamas and emus. That takes a little while. There are a number of cottages here with wood stoves, so in the winter I also fill up the stoves. Then I come home and feed Max and Lola, the dogs. We go for long walks in the woods. Walking them really clears my head.

When did the animals start having such a prominent role? ✳ LARRY: We've always had chickens, for the eggs. Early on I was involved with the insect life. I had thousands of praying mantises in the fields, which I would photograph. But when the birds came— the turkeys, the guinea hens, the peacocks, and all the other squawky elements—that was the end of the mantises' reign, because the birds ate them. The llamas were the first mammals to inhabit this territory, followed by the sheep and the goats.

How did you come to acquire the llamas? ✳ LARRY: I started to make a bit of money, and I had a taste for something exotic. Same thing with the emus and the peacocks. I wanted to surround myself with wild things. ✳ I don't like people as much as I like birds. Both Martha's and my minds work like any good Buddhist's, which we're not, but…We believe that the creatures that inhabit this earth are as important as we are, and they deserve as much consideration. We have all sorts of natural phenomena around us—things we watch grow slowly—that are full of the magic of their own creation.

How do you feel toward the animals? ✴ MARTHA: We used to have a bunch of different goats, and I loved them very much. They used to jump over the fence and come to have coffee with me on the porch in the morning. LeAnn in particular would hang out in front of my studio, and I would take little walks with this lovely goat named Violet. The goats we have now are very dear too, though I'm not as attached to them as I was to the first group. Part of it is just because every year we expand the gardens, and the farm gets busier and busier. I do love my beasts, though.

What are some of the things that you grow here? ✴ MARTHA: I grow what I want to eat: tomatoes, first and foremost—we grow seven different types; lots and lots of grains; every herb you can think of, and a few you can't; cabbages; cucumbers; edible flowers; peppers; a variety of chilies; beans; bok choy; Brussels sprouts; broccoli; Swiss chard. We grow a ton of stuff, really. I love that I can eat out of my garden and feed the people I love.

Tell me about the need to have plants inside your house when you're surrounded by nature? ✴ LARRY: That's my way. Martha is a great gardener, but I tend to the indoor plants. There are a couple of plants and trees that have been with me now for forty-three years. Old pals, man, old pals. One of them—a rock fig—was in a greenhouse accident, but I kept the pot. I really liked that damn plant and the person who gave it to me. Four years later, out of this decrepit old stump came this miracle of life. I said, "Oh, look at this. Here comes somebody!" That's dedication for you.

What do your visitors think when they come here? ✳ MARTHA: We have people stay almost every weekend. Most people who come here have come many times now, but when you have somebody visit for the first time, the experience is a little bit different. I would never let anyone wash a dish, for example, the first time they showed up at my house. But the first thing people respond to is that it's not quiet, because there are so many birds, and birds are noisy. Roosters don't only crow in the morning: if there's a full moon, they'll crow all night. ✳ LARRY: Everybody is always talking about the magic—the transformative magic—of the place. There are so many different elements—the animals, the plants, the little nooks and crannies. And we have a lot of stuff. It's not particularly valuable, but it's all over the place, and it's all sculpted together in an organic way so that everything talks to everything else. You can think of it as the spiritualization of material things that matter, because each thing that we have is part of our energy force. When people come and see all of this, they have a profound perceptual experience. We like that about the place.

Tell me about the decor. Are a lot of the things from your travels? ✳ LARRY: Some of our things, like the masks, are from Martha's travels to Mexico. But most of it is stuff that we've acquired over the years. Martha, of all of the people that I've been with in my life, has brought the most to me in terms of her ethics and her mythic interests. She is the one who brought color to the house. I've always pretty much been a white walls kind of guy, but she wanted to give the place other kinds of possibilities, and I went with it. She's been the one who has really been able to enter the most deeply into my life, and henceforth the house looks of her, and is of her, and is unbelievably magical because of her. She's a contender.

You can think of it as the

SPIRITUALIZATION OF MATERIAL THINGS

that matter, because

each thing that we have

IS PART OF OUR ENERGY FORCE.

—LARRY FINK

How do you feel when you come home to the farm after being in New York City? ✳ LARRY: I feel dissociated, because I deal with very sophisticated people—fast-moving types—on photo shoots there. I have to readjust to the smooth, intrinsic ways of the animals. I'm not hiding here, but this is a place where I can be peaceful. The farm releases me from the tensions and pretenses of professional life, even as it possibly distances me from certain opportunities that would come from being in the city all the time.

Do you think you're a healthier person for living here, in nature, at the farm? ✳ MARTHA: There's something about living a physical life that clearly appeals to us. I also like that it makes my work just part of what I do. Some artists in New York feel like they're so special because they make art. I mean, you make art, or you cook dinner, or you teach children, or whatever it is you do. You do it because it's within you to do it. It makes you unique, but it doesn't make you special. There's a big difference there. Here, working in the garden, or walking the dogs, or shoveling shit out of the barn doesn't seem all that different from working in my studio. It just seems like one more component of what I do.

What do you cherish about living at the farm? ✳ LARRY: I cherish most of all being absolutely alone. I can walk here or there without seeing anyone and without anything in my way. I also cherish the beauty. When I first came, it was a barren place, like farms usually are, and over the years I've helped it grow into the oasis it is now. ✳ MARTHA: Well, every now and then I think I don't want to do it any more. I say I want to live in a place where you walk in, and it's warm, and you don't have to put wood in the stove. But as soon as I drive down that road—that beautiful road that cuts through the forest—I think, "How could I live anywhere else?" ■